I Am Your Flag

by Chase Tunbridge

ISBN: 978-1-59577-080-6

Starfall Education
P.O. Box 359, Boulder, Colorado 80306

I am the flag of the United **States** of America. I belong to every American.

The Birth of Old Glory, Percy Moran

I was born June 14, 1777, in Philadelphia.

You celebrate my birthday every year,
on Flag Day.

The Thirteen Colonies

Massachusetts (Maine)

New York

Mass.

New Hampshire

Rhode Island
Connecticut

Pennsylvania

New Jersey

Delaware

Maryland

Virginia

North Carolina

South Carolina

Georgia

When I was young I had thirteen white stars, one for each of the first thirteen colonies, in a field of blue.

The color blue stands for the **union** of the thirteen states.

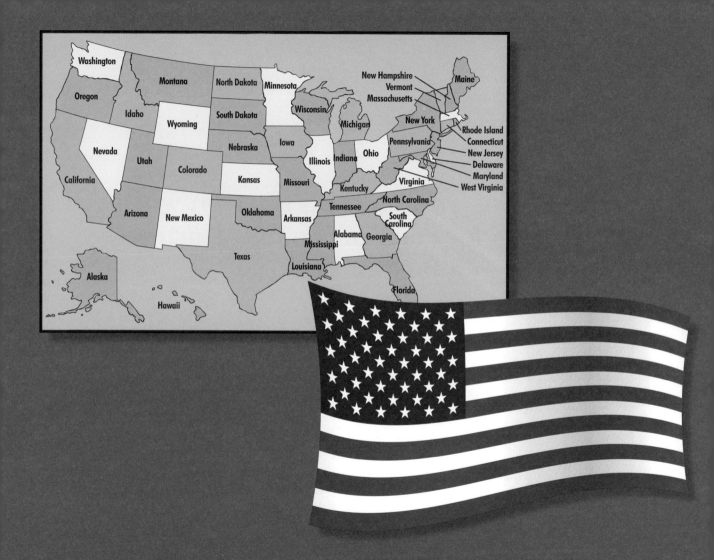

Today I have fifty stars! One star for each state in the union.

I have grown with our **nation**.

Washington Crossing the Delaware, Emanuel Leutze

My red stripes stand for **courage**.

My white stripes stand for **liberty**.

I love to fly. You'll see me outside of your school and the post office.

I am here to remind you of your freedom.

I am a **symbol** of the people of
the United States of America.

I am your flag.

Glossary

Courage: Able to face a challenge without letting fear stop you

Liberty: Freedom to choose

Nation: A large group of people with a single national government

State: A piece of land within a nation that has borders, people, and government

Symbol: A picture that stands for an idea: for example, a heart is a symbol for love

Union: A group of states united or joined together to form a nation: for example, The United States of America

The History of *The Pledge of Allegiance*

1892

Francis Bellamy wrote the original Pledge of Allegiance for a magazine advertising campaign celebrating the 400th anniversary of Columbus arriving in the Americas. The original Pledge read:

I Pledge allegiance to my Flag
and the Republic for which it stands:
one Nation indivisible, with
Liberty and Justice for all.

The Pledge was first recited in public schools in 1892 during Columbus Day observances.

1945

The Pledge was not adopted by the U.S. Congress as our official national pledge until December 28, 1945. The first adopted Pledge read:

I Pledge allegiance to the Flag,
of the United States of America,
and to the Republic for which it stands:
one Nation indivisible, with
Liberty and Justice for all.

Although it is our national pledge, no one is required to say it.

1954

In 1954 President Eisenhower heard a sermon that emphasized adding the words "under God" to the Pledge. President Eisenhower was so moved by the sermon that he successfully urged Congress to change the Pledge to the one we know today:

I Pledge allegiance to the Flag,
of the United States of America,
and to the Republic for which it stands:
one Nation, under God, indivisible,
with Liberty and Justice for all.

Can you find your state flag?

Alabama

Arizona

Florida

Iowa

Massachusetts

Nebraska

North Carolina

Rhode Island

Vermont

Arkansas

Georgia

Kansas

Michigan

Nevada

North Dakota

South Carolina

Virginia

California

Hawaii

Kentucky

Minnesota

New Hampshire

Ohio

South Dakota

Washington

Colorado

Idaho

Louisiana

Mississippi

New Jersey

Oklahoma

Tennessee

West Virginia

Connecticut

Illinois

Maine

Missouri

New Mexico

Oregon

Texas

Wisconsin

Alaska

Delaware

Indiana

Maryland

Montana

New York

Pennsylvania

Utah

Wyoming